RHODE ISLAND

EXPLORE THE UNITED STATES

Sara

Big Buddy BOOKS

VISIT US AT
www.abdopublishing.com

Published by ABDO Publishing Company, PO Box 398166, Minneapolis, MN 55439.

Printed in the United States of America, North Mankato, Minnesota.
052012
092012

♻ PRINTED ON RECYCLED PAPER

Coordinating Series Editor: Rochelle Baltzer
Contributing Editors: Megan M. Gunderson, Marcia Zappa
Graphic Design: Adam Craven
Cover Photograph: *Shutterstock*: Stuart Monk.
Interior Photographs/Illustrations: *Alamy*: David R. Frazier Photolibrary, Inc. (p. 19), North Wind Picture Archives (p. 13), George Oze (p. 25); *AP Photo*: Stew Mine (p. 23), Stew Mine, File (p. 19), National Portrait Gallery (p. 25), Mary Schwalm (p. 27); *Getty Images*: CHRIS BJORNBERG/Photo Researchers (p. 30); *iStockphoto*: ©iStockphoto.com/gmcoop (p. 9), ©iStockphoto.com/SDbt (pp. 27, 29), ©iStockphoto.com/sphraner (p. 27), ©iStockphoto.com/DenisTangneyJr (pp. 21, 26), ©iStockphoto.com/Turbinado (p. 30); *Shutterstock*: 2happy (p. 25), ARENA Creative (p. 17), Melinda Fawver (p. 30), Eric Full (p. 5), K. L. Kohn (p. 9), Philip Lange (p. 30), littleny (p. 26), Anthony Ricci (p. 11).

All population figures taken from the 2010 US census.

Library of Congress Cataloging-in-Publication Data

Tieck, Sarah, 1976-
  Rhode Island / Sarah Tieck.
     p. cm. -- (Explore the United States)
  ISBN 978-1-61783-378-6
  1. Rhode Island--Juvenile literature. I. Title.
  F79.3.T54 2013
  974.5--dc23
                                2012016391

Contents

ONE NATION

The United States is a **diverse** country. It has farmland, cities, coasts, and mountains. Its people come from many different backgrounds. And, its history covers more than 200 years.

Today the country includes 50 states. Rhode Island is one of these states. Let's learn more about this state and its story!

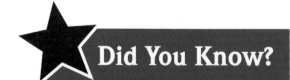

Did You Know?

Rhode Island became a state on May 29, 1790. It was the thirteenth state to join the nation.

Rhode Island is on the Atlantic Ocean. It has about 400 miles (640 km) of coastline!

5

Rhode Island Up Close

The United States has four main **regions**. Rhode Island is in the Northeast.

Rhode Island has two states on its borders. Connecticut is west. Massachusetts is north and east. The Atlantic Ocean is south.

Rhode Island is the smallest state. It has a total area of 1,221 square miles (3,162 sq km). About 1 million people live there.

Did You Know?

Washington DC is the US capital city. Puerto Rico is a US commonwealth. This means it is governed by its own people.

REGIONS OF THE UNITED STATES

= West
= Midwest
= South
= Northeast

CANADA

WASHINGTON
MONTANA
NORTH DAKOTA
MINNESOTA
VERMONT
MAINE
NEW HAMPSHIRE
MASSACHUSETTS
OREGON
WISCONSIN
NEW YORK
RHODE ISLAND
CONNECTICUT
IDAHO
WYOMING
SOUTH DAKOTA
MICHIGAN
PENNSYLVANIA
NEW JERSEY
IOWA
OHIO
NEVADA
NEBRASKA
INDIANA
Washington DC ★
DELAWARE
MARYLAND
WEST VIRGINIA
PACIFIC OCEAN
UTAH
COLORADO
ILLINOIS
VIRGINIA
CALIFORNIA
KANSAS
MISSOURI
KENTUCKY
NORTH CAROLINA
ATLANTIC OCEAN
ARIZONA
OKLAHOMA
ARKANSAS
TENNESSEE
SOUTH CAROLINA
NEW MEXICO
MISSISSIPPI
GEORGIA
TEXAS
LOUISIANA
ALABAMA
FLORIDA
GULF OF MEXICO
ALASKA
MEXICO
HAWAII
PUERTO RICO

N
W E
S

IMPORTANT CITIES

   Providence is Rhode Island's **capital**. It is also the state's largest city, with 178,042 people. This important port city is located at the head of Narragansett Bay. The Providence River flows into the bay.

   Providence is known for its history. It was founded in 1636. It was one of the first places to allow **religious freedom**.

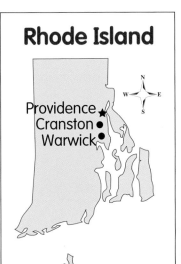

Rhode Island

Providence
Cranston
Warwick

The Rhode Island State House is known for its large marble dome.

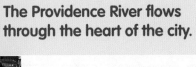

The Providence River flows through the heart of the city.

9

Warwick is the second-largest city in Rhode Island. It has 82,672 people. It is on the shores of Narragansett Bay.

Cranston is the state's third-largest city, with 80,387 people. It is on the Pawtuxet River. Both Warwick and Cranston are part of the Providence **metropolitan** area.

The first Warwick Lighthouse was built in the 1820s. It was replaced in the 1930s.

Rhode Island in History

Rhode Island's history includes Native Americans and war. Native Americans have lived in present-day Rhode Island for thousands of years.

In 1524, an Italian explorer was the first European to visit the area. English colonists arrived in the 1630s. They wanted to live somewhere that provided **religious freedom**.

In 1775, colonists fought in the **Revolutionary War**. This led to the forming of the United States. Rhode Island became a state on May 29, 1790.

The Rhode Island colony was started by a minister named Roger Williams.

13

Timeline

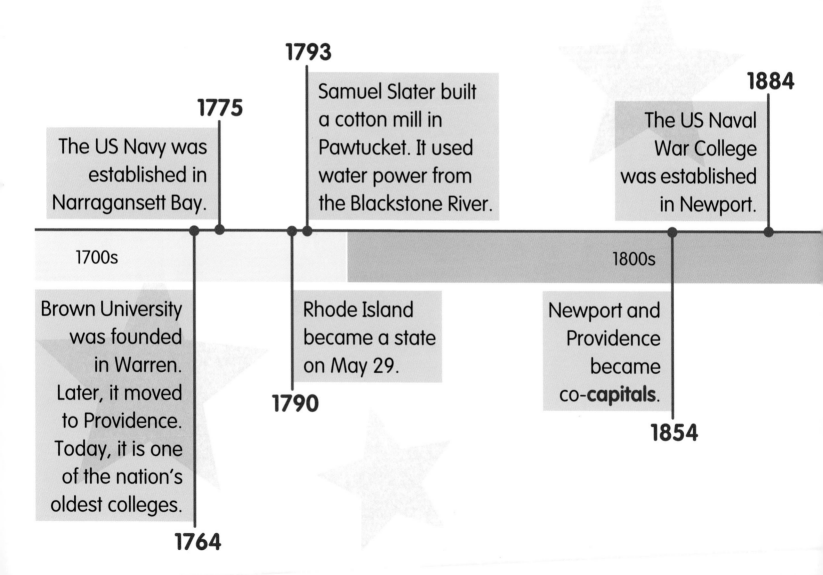

1793

Samuel Slater built a cotton mill in Pawtucket. It used water power from the Blackstone River.

1775

The US Navy was established in Narragansett Bay.

1884

The US Naval War College was established in Newport.

1700s

1800s

Brown University was founded in Warren. Later, it moved to Providence. Today, it is one of the nation's oldest colleges.

Rhode Island became a state on May 29.

1790

Newport and Providence became co-**capitals**.

1854

1764

1900

Providence became Rhode Island's only **capital**.

1938

A **hurricane** struck Rhode Island. This was one of the state's worst natural disasters. More than 300 people died, and buildings were harmed.

2010

The Pawtuxet and other rivers in the state rose to record-high levels after heavy rains. Many homes and businesses were flooded.

1900s

2000s

The Claiborne Pell Bridge was built over Narragansett Bay. Most people call it the Newport Bridge. It brought more visitors to the state.

The annual Newport Jazz Festival celebrated 50 years.

2004

1969

15

ACROSS THE LAND

Rhode Island has beaches, hills, forests, and islands. At 812 feet (248 m), Jerimoth Hill is the highest point in the state. Major rivers include the Providence, Blackstone, and Pawtuxet. Narragansett Bay is in southeastern Rhode Island.

Many types of animals make their homes in this state. These include owls, beavers, and trout.

Did You Know?

In July, the average temperature in Rhode Island is 71°F (22°C). In January, it is 29°F (-2°C).

Rhode Island has more than 30 islands! The largest one is called Rhode Island, just like the state. But, many people call it Aquidneck.

Earning a Living

Rhode Island has many important businesses. Some people work for finance or **real estate** companies. Others have jobs helping visitors to the state. Rhode Island is also known for manufacturing jewelry. And people catch lobsters, clams, and squid in the state's coastal waters.

Hasbro toy company is based in Pawtucket. It makes Mr. Potato Head toys!

Rhode Island's farms provide sod, trees, and other plants for yards and gardens.

Natural Wonder

Narragansett Bay is one of Rhode Island's natural wonders. It starts at the Atlantic Ocean and goes 28 miles (45 km) inland. Most of the state's islands are within this bay.

Many people visit Narragansett Bay for vacations. They go boating and fishing in its waters.

The Newport Harbor Lighthouse in Narragansett Bay was first built in the 1800s. It guides boats near the Newport Bridge.

HOMETOWN HEROES

Many famous people have lived in Rhode Island. Roger Williams was born in London, England, around 1603. He founded the city of Providence and the colony of Rhode Island.

Williams was a minister. He believed in **religious freedom**. In 1636, he started a settlement for people who also believed in this. Over time, the settlement became the city of Providence.

Williams was the president of the Rhode Island colony from 1654 to 1657.

Gilbert Stuart was born in present-day North Kingstown in 1755. He grew up in Newport. Stuart was famous for his art.

Stuart first started painting around age 13. He studied art with master teachers for many years. In 1782, his painting called *The Skater* caught people's attention. After this, Stuart made a living painting pictures of wealthy people.

Stuart painted more than 1,000 pictures of people. One famous painting was of George Washington (*right*). Today, it appears on the US one-dollar bill.

Today, people can visit the Gilbert Stuart Birthplace and Museum.

Tour Book

Do you want to go to Rhode Island? If you visit the state, here are some places to go and things to do!

★ Taste

Eat some squid (*left*) or clams! Rhode Island is known for being a source of seafood.

★ Remember

See Slater Mill in Pawtucket. This was the first successful cotton mill in the United States. It dates to 1793.

26

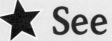 ## See

Watch boaters in Narragansett Bay. Many people sail in these waters.

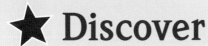 ## Discover

Visit the Roger Williams Park Zoo in Providence. It is home to more than 100 different types of animals! The zoo opened in 1872.

 ## Walk

Explore Newport's famous Cliff Walk along the Atlantic Ocean. The path goes past historic mansions, such as the Breakers (*left*).

A Great State

The story of Rhode Island is important to the United States. The people and places that make up this state offer something special to the country. Together with all the states, Rhode Island helps make the United States great.

The Cliff Walk is one of the state's popular places to visit. In some parts, people walk over cliffs along the ocean!

29

Fast Facts

Date of Statehood:
May 29, 1790

Population (rank):
1,052,567
(43rd most-populated state)

Total Area (rank):
1,221 square miles
(50th largest state)

Motto:
Hope

Nickname:
Little Rhody,
Ocean State

State Capital:
Providence

Flag:

Flower: Blue Violet

Postal Abbreviation:
RI

Tree: Red Maple

Bird: Rhode Island Red
Chicken

Important Words

capital a city where government leaders meet.

diverse made up of things that are different from each other.

hurricane a tropical storm that forms over seawater with strong winds, rain, thunder, and lightning.

metropolitan of or relating to a large city, usually with nearby smaller cities called suburbs.

real estate the business of selling buildings and land.

region a large part of a country that is different from other parts.

religious freedom the freedom to pray and worship as one chooses.

Revolutionary War a war fought between England and the North American colonies from 1775 to 1783.

Web Sites

To learn more about Rhode Island, visit ABDO Publishing Company online. Web sites about Rhode Island are featured on our Book Links page. These links are routinely monitored and updated to provide the most current information available.

www.abdopublishing.com

Index